LIFE IN THE U.S. NAVY

by Mari Bolte

PEBBLE
a capstone imprint

Published by Pebble, an imprint of Capstone
1710 Roe Crest Drive, North Mankato, Minnesota 56003
capstonepub.com

Copyright © 2025 by Capstone. All rights reserved. No part of this publication may be reproduced in whole or in part, or stored in a retrieval system, or transmitted in any form or by any means, electronic, mechanical, photocopying, recording, or otherwise, without written permission of the publisher.

Library of Congress Cataloging-in-Publication Data is available on the Library of Congress website.

ISBN: 9780756579920 (hardcover)
ISBN: 9780756580247 (paperback)
ISBN: 9780756579944 (ebook PDF)

Summary: Gives readers a peak into daily life for members of the U.S. Navy.

Editorial Credits
Editor: Mandy Robbins; Designer: Heidi Thompson; Media Researcher: Jo Miller; Production Specialist: Tori Abraham

Image Credits
Getty Images: supersizer, 21; Shutterstock: Glynnis Jones, 19, Picksell, Cover, background (throughout); U.S. Navy photo by Mass Communication Specialist (MC) 1st Class Brian McNeal, 18, MC 1st Class Fred Gray IV, 16, MC 1st Class Jeffrey M. Richardson, 13, MC 2nd Class Austin Haist, 7, MC 2nd Class Diana Quinlan, Cover, (bottom), MC 2nd Class Jackson Adkins, 8, MC 2nd Class Justin Stumberg, 11, MC 3rd Class Anthony N. Hilkowski, 9, MC 3rd Class Gerald Dudley Reynolds, 15, MC 3rd Class Kelsey J. Hockenberger, Cover, (top left), MC 3rd Class Taylor Crenshaw, 17, MC Seaman Apprentice Carson J. Davis, Cover, (top right), Michael Meyers, Cover, (top middle), Petty Officer 3rd Class Stephen D. Doyle II, 5; Wikimedia: U.S. Navy photo by Photographer's Mate 2nd Class Jayme Pastoric, 10

The appearance of U.S. Department of Defense (DoD) visual information does not imply or constitute DoD endorsement.

Any additional websites and resources referenced in this book are not maintained, authorized, or sponsored by Capstone. All product and company names are trademarks™ or registered® trademarks of their respective holders.

TABLE OF CONTENTS

Land, Sea, and Sky.....................4

Life on Land............................6

Assignment: Aircraft Carrier............8

Life Underwater.......................12

Mission Time..........................14

Sleep Like a Sailor....................20

    Glossary...........................22

    Read More.........................23

    Internet Sites.....................23

    Index..............................24

    About the Author..................24

Words in **bold** appear in the glossary.

LAND, SEA, AND SKY

The U.S. Navy protects the land, sea, and sky. Sailors, officers, and their families live all over the world. Some sailors even stay on ships or in **submarines**.

Those who serve must be ready for **combat** at any moment. Keeping people safe around the world is a big responsibility.

The Abraham Lincoln Carrier Strike Group

LIFE ON LAND

People who work for the U.S. Navy can live and work on a **base**. Bases are just like towns. They have post offices. There is a fire station. Doctors, dentists, and businesses are nearby.

Families live in houses or apartments. There are also military buildings nearby.

The Naval base in San Diego, California

ASSIGNMENT: AIRCRAFT CARRIER

Around 50,000 sailors live on ships around the world. They might spend a couple months at sea. Others spend three to six years there! Sailors are ready to attack or defend against enemies.

The USS Gerald R. Ford

Aircraft carriers are the biggest type of Naval ship. They are also called "cities at sea." Around 5,000 to 6,000 people live together on board.

The USS *Theodore Roosevelt*

Most sailors sleep on small **bunks**. Everyone gets a storage bin and a locker. They can keep their clothing and belongings there. Officers get a little more space and privacy. There are few bathrooms. Sailors have to share.

Sailors eat together in mess halls. They exercise in gyms. They watch TV and relax in lounges.

LIFE UNDERWATER

Sailors spend months underwater on submarines. Sub life can be hard. Around 120 crew members squeeze into a tight space. There are strict limits on internet and cell phone use. There are no windows.

Sailors may even have to share bunks. "Hot racking" means three sailors share two beds. They work and sleep during different shifts. But working that closely means sailors form tight friendships.

Bunks on a submarine

MISSION TIME

Missions might take sailors into dangerous places. Everyone on board a ship or sub must be ready for action at all times.

Sailors work and sleep in shifts. When they're doing their jobs, they're "on watch."

Sailors on watch on the USS *San Diego*

There are many jobs on a naval ship. Airplanes may need **pilots**. Ships need to be steered. Machines and computers need to be fixed. Cooks prepare meals.

Both physical and mental health are important. Doctors and nurses keep everyone healthy.

"Off watch" means it's time to take a break. There are many ways sailors can relax. Relaxing is even more fun when naval ships **dock** on shore.

Naval bases are places where ships stop for repairs and fresh supplies. Sailors can get off the ship. There are bases all over the world. Sailors can shop or eat. Trying new foods can be fun! Friends and family can even come to visit.

SLEEP LIKE A SAILOR

Bunks on a Navy ship are small. Create your own "bunk," and imagine this is your living space for months.

Cover a rectangular table with a bedsheet. The sheet should cover three sides of the table. Leave one long side open. Tape the sheet in place. Pack some personal belongings in a backpack. The backpack is about as much storage space as a sailor gets on board a ship.

GLOSSARY

aircraft carrier (AIR-kraft CARE-ee-uhr)—a ship that carries planes and helicopters and that has a runway on deck for takeoffs and landings

base (BAYS)—an area run by the military where people serving in the military live and military supplies are stored

bunk (BUHNGK)—a narrow bed, often stacked

combat (KOM-bat)—fighting between militaries

dock (DAHK)—when a ship stops on land in order for people to go from ship to shore or shore to ship

pilot (PYE-luht)—a person who operates a flying vehicle

submarine (SUHB-muh-reen)—a ship that can travel both on the surface of and under the water

READ MORE

Besel, Jennifer M. *U.S. Navy*. Mankato, MN: Black Rabbit Books, 2023.

Conaghan, Bernard. *Navy*. New York: Crabtree Publishing, 2023.

Schuh, Mari C. *Military Ships and Submarines*. North Mankato, MN: Pebble, an imprint of Capstone, 2023.

INTERNET SITES

Encyclopedia Britannica: Navy
kids.britannica.com/students/article/navy/276044

Kiddle: United States Navy Facts for Kids
kids.kiddle.co/United_States_Navy

U.S. Navy: For Families
navy.com/what-to-expect/for-families

INDEX

aircraft carriers, 5, 8, 9
airplanes, 16

bases, 6, 7, 19
bunks, 10, 12, 13, 20

exercises, 11

hot racking, 12

jobs, 14, 16

mess halls, 11
missions, 14

shifts, 12, 14
submarines, 4, 12, 14

ABOUT THE AUTHOR

Mari Bolte is the author and editor of hundreds of children's books. Every book is her favorite book as long as the readers learned something and enjoyed themselves!